Edward P. Heizer

Sioux City illustrated;

The pioneer period and an authentic sketch of the Sioux City of today

Edward P. Heizer

Sioux City illustrated;
The pioneer period and an authentic sketch of the Sioux City of today

ISBN/EAN: 9783337727826

Printed in Europe, USA, Canada, Australia, Japan

Cover: Foto ©ninafisch / pixelio.de

More available books at **www.hansebooks.com**

Sioux City Illustrated:

THE PIONEER PERIOD

AND AN AUTHENTIC SKETCH OF

THE SIOUX CITY OF TO-DAY

EMBRACING

The Stages of Its Development and Relation to the
Upper Missouri Valley,

WITH

OVER SIXTY ILLUSTRATIONS, AND AN ARTICLE ON THE FAMOUS CORN PALACE.

———

EDITED BY E. P. HEIZER.

SIOUX CITY, AND OMAHA,
D. C. DUNBAR & COMPANY, PUBLISHERS.
1888.

PERKINS BROS. CO., PRINTERS AND BINDERS, SIOUX CITY, IOWA.

THE SIOUX CITY CORN PALACE: SECOND ANNUAL FESTIVAL
SEPTEMBER 24th TO OCTOBER 5th, 1888.

EARLY HISTORY.

THE PIONEER PERIOD OF SIOUX CITY.

HISTORY of Sioux City may be conveniently considered in two distinct epochs, viz.: the period during which it was connected with the movement of trade and settlement which pierced the Northwest, following the waterway of the Missouri River; and the later period during which its growth has been determined by the comprehensive transfer of population, effected by the building of railroads westwardly. The former epoch began with the arrival, in June, 1856, of the first steamboat freighted for Sioux City, which, that year, grew to be a town of 400 inhabitants; it may be said to close with the completion of the first railroad, in March, 1868.

All that goes before—and it would make a chapter of romantic story—relates to the time of pure adventure in the northwest, rather than to its substantial development; it includes the day of exploration, of the French voyageur, of the trader and the trapper.

The first account of the visit of white men to Woodbury County is that of the famous exploring expedition of Lewis and Clark, in 1804. This is immortalized by the names they gave to localities, and one spot is sacred as the last resting place of the first of their number who fell during the expedition. On the 20th of August, 1804, Sergt. Charles Floyd died and was buried by his comrades on a high bluff overlooking the Missouri River. The grave is still to be seen on the bluff which bears his name, and his memory has a more enduring record in the Floyd River, which, passing through the city limits of Sioux City, empties into the Missouri two miles above this bluff.

In the summer of 1848, a single pioneer, William Thompson, settled at Floyd's Bluff, his brother and another man joining him in the fall. Next year he laid out a town there, calling it Thompsonville. Thompson's cabin was the sole improvement, but on the organization of the county, in 1853, the ville was made the county seat, and it was a sort of post for Indian traders for some years. Not a vestige of Thompsonville remains.

In May, 1849, Theophili Brughier, a French Canadian, settled at the mouth of the Big Sioux two miles above the original Sioux City, but now within the city limits—the most beautiful spot in the

VIEWS IN HIGHLAND AND RIVERSIDE PARKS.

northwest, and known as Riverside Park. Brughier had been in the employ of the American Fur Company, but leaving them and joining the Yankton Sioux Indians he married the daughter of their celebrated chief, War Eagle. He acquired great influence among the Indians, and War Eagle died at his house in 1851. The remains of the old chief, with those of his daughter, Brughier's wife, and several others of the family, now repose on the summit of a lofty bluff near the mouth of the Big Sioux River, within the present city limits.

The next two settlers of 1849 were Robert Perry, who settled on the creek which bears his name, flowing now through the heart of the city, and Paul Pacquette, who settled on the Big Sioux.

In the spring of 1852, Joseph Leonias purchased of Brughier the quarter section on which the business portion of Sioux City is now built.

BIRD'S EYE VIEW UNION STOCK YARDS.

1—Booge Packing House.   2—Fowler Packing House.   3—Silberhorn Packing House.   4—Proposed Swift Packing House.
5 South Sioux City.   6 Morning Side Addition.   7—Exchange Building.

There was no further improvement until 1854, when Dr. John K. Cook, who had a contract under the government to survey a part of Northwestern Iowa, landed here. Refusing to be intimidated by a band of Indians under Smutty Bear, their chief, who were encamped here, Dr. Cook, impressed with the commercial importance of the site and the beauty of the surroundings, boldly located a claim, as did several of his party, and began to lay out Sioux City in December, 1854. Dr. Cook's claim and the original town site lay on the west side of Perry Creek, but the next spring he purchased of Joseph Leonias his quarter section and laid out Sioux City East addition.

It would require more space than there is at command to chronicle the interesting events of the next few years. Indians frequently passed through the town in war paint, and uttering whoops, sometimes admonishing the settlers to leave, but no violence or bloodshed occurred. In the spring of 1855 there were two log cabins on the site of Sioux City. In July of this year the first stage and mail arrived. Dr. Cook was the first postmaster. Before the close of 1855 there were seven log houses, two being hotels. There were two stores, one in a tent and the other in a log cabin. A land office was opened for pre-emption, but not for sale till May, 1857. The County Seat was removed here from Floyd's Bluff, or Thompsonville, in 1856. Sioux City was incorporated by an Act of the Legislature, approved January 16, 1857, and the first city election took place August 31, 1857. The first newspaper was edited by Seth W. Swiggett. It was called the Sioux City Eagle and was first issued July 4, 1857.

As before stated, the first steamboat, freighted for Sioux City, arrived in June, 1856, bringing provisions and ready-framed houses. The base of supplies was then, and for years after, St. Louis, and transportation was by way of the Missouri River. The commanding commercial relation of Sioux City to the great Northwest, even at that early day, was clearly perceived, since from it, as a depot, freights were

BOOGE PACKING CO.'S PLANT.

distributed by water carriage to the trading posts, government stations, and scattered settlements of the upper Missouri valley. This was the original *raison d'eter* of Sioux City. At its inception it was a depot and distributing center to the Northwest.

During 1856 the population increased to 400, and about ninety buildings were erected.

It must be remembered that this was before the day of railroad development west of the Mississippi River. Two or three weak lines had been constructed for short distances west of that river, but their progress was slow. The Pacific railroads were yet far in the future. Chicago, even, was yet in its day of small things, and the settlement of the upper Mississippi valley, from which Chicago later fed its majestic strength, was only in its beginnings. The upper Missouri valley, opening above Sioux City, was still a primeval wilderness, still to be disputed with the countless bands of Indians and buffalo which roamed over it.

But Sioux City grew steadily with the extension of settlement westwardly. It is needless now to recount the various stages of growth by which, in 1868, the advent of the first railroad, it reached a population of 1,030. This was the day of the steamboat, the stage, the freighter's wagon. While these things remained many years after the opening of the first railroad—notably during the four years, beginning in 1875, when the Black Hills mines were discovered,—yet the advent of the railroad in 1868 revolutionized the movement of trade through Sioux City to the Northwest, finally fixing the base

R. D. FOWLER PACKING CO.'S PLANT.

of supply at Chicago instead of at St. Louis. The change marked a new era in the history both of Sioux City and the Northwest; it involved for them an ampler and more energetic development.

But the material fact indicated by the history of the old era, as well as of the new, is the commercial identity of Sioux City with the upper Missouri valley, whether the distribution of supplies was effected from St. Louis or from Chicago as the base.

SIOUX CITY OF TO-DAY.

On the site of Dr. Cook's claim in 1854, and the additions thereto since made, there is now a city of 30,000 inhabitants. Such change from a pioneer settlement to a commanding trade center is a transition which could occur only in the west.

It is not the intention here to describe in detail the Sioux City of to-day, but rather to reserve space for some exposition of the logic of its situation. A few representative facts, however, may be briefly summarized.

SILBERHORN PACKING CO'S. PLANT.

The Sioux City of the railroad epoch, beginning in 1868, when the Sioux City & Pacific Railroad was opened to Missouri Valley, seventy miles south, making connection there with an east and west railroad, shared the rising enthusiasm of the Northwest, and grew steadily. During the next few years enterprising men projected lines of road into the region about Sioux City northwardly with a view to ultimate connection with the Northern Pacific, northwesterly through Southern Dakota, and directly west through Northern Nebraska from the opposite shore of the Missouri. Nearly all these routes have been since occupied by trunk or branch lines radiating from Sioux City, but then there was success in building only a few spurs, when railroad enterprise was smitten with the general industrial paralysis which followed the great failure of Jay Cooke & Co., in 1873.

But, Sioux City growing steadily, had a population of 4,290 in 1875, and the federal census of 1880 showed an increase to 7,366 inhabitants. The state census of 1885, fixed the population then at

19,060, and a census taken eighteen months later, including territory since added by the extension of the corporate limits, showed a population of 26,000.

The notable growth of Sioux City, it will be seen, has been since 1880, and in fact 20,000 of the 30,000 of its present population have been drawn hither since 1882.

Sioux City, to-day, is the center of five great trunk lines of railway which have thirteen main and branch lines diverging hence, through Northern Iowa, Southern Minnesota, Nebraska, Dakota, Wyoming and Montana. These companies have machine shops here and a railroad bridge across the Missouri River, costing $1,250,000, is approaching completion. Thirty-six passenger trains arrive and depart daily.

The largest jobbing center in Iowa, Sioux City is also the largest jobbing center in the Northwest,

SIOUX CITY PLOW CO.—OFFICE AND WORKS.

filling its own distinct field and competing with Omaha on the one hand and Minneapolis and St. Paul on the other. All the principal lines of jobbing are represented. The sales for 1887 amounted to over $8,500,000. Two hundred commercial travelers represent the city in the tributary territory. While within half a decade population has quadrupled, business has increased eightfold.

The total expenditures for building improvements during 1887, on a careful and accurate basis of ascertainment, were $2,854,856; for 1886, $1,292,528; for 1885, $1,024,471; for 1884, $980,395; for 1883, $660,949; for 1882, $637,324.

There are nine banking houses, with a capital of $2,000,000, which in 1887 sold exchange to the amount of $57,000,000—a banking interest exceeding that of any other city in Iowa. The postal receipts in 1887 were $46,017, against $32,211 in 1886, while the money order business was $951,315.46, an increase of 30 per cent. over 1886. The telegraph business is the largest in the Northwest, there being a remarkable increase during the past two years, while the business of the three express companies represented here has trebled during the same period.

Sioux City is one of the five greatest packing centers in the United States. There are three great packing establishments—those of Booge, Silberhorn, and Fowler. These have a capacity of 15,000 hogs and 2,000 beeves per day. In addition, it is practically assured that one of the largest dressed beef establishments in the world will be located and built here during the passing year.

OFFICE AND WAREROOMS SIOUX CITY CRACKER AND CANDY CO.

The Stock Yards, in the vicinity of which the packing houses are situated, are one of the most important factors in Sioux City's growth. They grew out of the concentration here of live-stock transactions, and, although founded less than three years ago, they have accommodations for 6,000 hogs, 10,000 cattle, 2,000 sheep, and 2,000 horses. Over $750,000 was expended last year in improving this property, and extensive improvements are being made this year. The yards include 1,400 acres of suburban land and 200 city lots.

In addition to the packing establishments, which give employment to hundreds of men, there are the Linseed Oil Mill—the second largest in the world—Flour Mills, Foundries, Machine Shops, Candy and Cracker Factory, Oatmeal Mill, Brick and Tile Works, Plow Works, Vinegar and Pickling Works, etc.

The public improvements are in harmony with Sioux City's progressive character, and yet so rapid is its growth that they are in rear of the public demand. In 1887 nearly a million dollars was expended in betterments of a purely public character, and a much larger sum will be expended this year. The city has sixty miles of graded streets, fifteen miles of cedar block paving, fourteen miles of street railway, and five of motor line in operation. Five miles of cable car line is projected for this season, while construction

SIOUX CITY VINEGAR AND PICKLING WORKS.

has begun on five miles of new motor line, which is to be connected with the business heart of the city by an elevated railway.

The city is located between three rivers, affording admirable drainage. This healthful situation is made perfect by the modern system of sewage.

Among other notable features the following few may be mentioned:

1. The finest water-works in the Northwest, consisting of two Holly-Gastel patent pumps of 4,000,000 gallons daily capacity, with reservoir of 1,500,000 gallons capacity and twenty-one miles of mains.

2. A paid professional fire department.

3. One of the finest Opera Houses in the West, almost completed.

4. The largest Telephone Exchange in Iowa.

5. Gas and Electric Lights, etc.

6. Four daily—one morning and three evening—papers, besides a variety of weekly and other periodicals.

7. An unrivalled system of public education; churches of all denominations; benevolent and charitable organizations; public library; Y. M. C. A. building (planned); Samaritan Home (hospital), maintained by the Women's Christian Association, etc., etc.

8. Sioux City Jobbers' and Manufacturers' Association, maintaining a salaried commissioner of freights, and the Chamber of Commerce Association.

SIOUX CITY FOUNDRY AND MACHINE WORKS.

Such are only a handful of facts chosen from a multitude of others because they are representative facts. From them may be inferred some idea of the scene of Sioux City as it is. But this further fact must be borne in mind: that, as two-thirds of Sioux City's 30,000 population has been added since 1882, so nearly all the great improvements above mentioned have been built up within the same short period. The oil mill has been built within four years; five banks within four; four new lines of railroad within two; the street cars within three and the motor line within a year-and-a-half; the water-works within two; all the paving within two; the stock-yards within two; while within the year just passed two of the three great packing establishments, the railroad bridge, the opera house, etc., have been secured.

The Sioux City of To-day and the Sioux City of Yesterday, the modern metropolis and the frontier settlement—where is there a broader contrast or a more magical transition?

SIOUX CITY'S SIGNIFICANCE.

RELATION TO THE UPPER MISSOURI VALLEY.

The logic of the situation of Sioux City must not be confounded with that of scores and hundreds of thriving towns in the west. The latter are, as a rule, as all but a comparatively few cities must be, essentially local. They are prosperous, but their trade and influence are circumscribed within a comparatively small territory.

SIOUX CITY BRICK AND TILE WORKS.

In bold contrast with the multitude of essentially local trading points of the west, Sioux City has been fashioned by the same class of forces which have built up Kansas City, Omaha, and Minneapolis and St. Paul, independent market cities and capitals of great trade empires of their own. To understand Sioux City is to understand the development of the upper Missouri valley. To have an adequate conception of the significance of Sioux City, requires first to appreciate that gigantic movement of population, which, within the past ten years, has transferred from the States north of the Ohio River, a million of population into the specific region because of whose growth Sioux City has grown. Just as Cincinnati grew to trade primacy in the Ohio valley with the advance of settlement from over the Alleghanies down that waterway; just as later the advance of railways westward from Chicago poured the wealth of Iowa, Wisconsin, Northern Illinois and Michigan into its lap, making it a wonder of growth and power; just as later the sudden out-reaching of railroads through Kansas and the Southwest made Kansas City; just as still later the building of the Union Pacific fed the strength of Omaha; just as the Northern Pacific and the Manitoba systems, tapping the wheat granary of the continent to the north, lifted Minneapolis and St. Paul—just so, to complete the whole field, have the new energies and developing resources of the upper Missouri valley at once required and created here the trade center which Sioux City is. The forces working to these great ends are indicated in all these cases, and the parallelism complete.

Consider some of the details of development of the tributary empire with which Sioux City has to do. Even to the distant observer the map suggests some of them.

OFFICE, MILL AND ELEVATOR—CITY MILL COMPANY.

Sioux City is situated at the point where the Missouri River makes the great bend to the west, just as at Kansas City it makes the great bend to the north. Precisely at Sioux City the drainage systems of Northwestern Iowa, Northern Nebraska and the whole of Southern Dakota converge. The Big Sioux River from due north, forming the boundary line between Iowa and Dakota, joins the Missouri, and the angle thus formed includes the west and south boundaries of the corporate limits of Sioux City. From the confluence with the Sioux River, the Missouri flows over 100 miles from almost due west, forming the boundary line between Dakota and Nebraska. The whole of the southeastern quarter of Dakota is drained by the James and Vermillion Rivers and innumerable smaller streams which flow almost due south, parallel to the Sioux, their fertile valleys debouching upon the Missouri at short distances above Sioux City. The drainage of Northern Nebraska is the exact complement of that of Southern Dakota, the Niobrara flowing northeast and joining the Missouri where it ceases to be the boundary line between Nebraska and Dakota, while from that point to Sioux City scores of minor streams flow northerly and northeasterly through Nebraska to a confluence with the Missouri. On the Iowa side the whole northwestern quarter of the State, with a portion of Minnesota, is drained into the Missouri at Sioux City, the Sioux River at its mouth forming its western boundary, as before stated, the Floyd River passing through the city limits, and the Little Sioux entering the Missouri at no great distance below.

Remember, now, that the trade territory of Sioux City in Northwestern Iowa alone is 8,000 square miles draining naturally, as in trade, to this point. Remember that Southern Dakota which opens northwestwardly from Sioux City as a gate, includes 60,000 square miles, while due west of Sioux City there is in Northern Nebraska 26,000 square miles. Here is a territory of 94,000 square miles which centers naturally and infallibly at Sioux City. And let it be borne in mind, moreover, that this territory, immense as it is, is only part of the territory now actually occupied or reached by Sioux City's trade.

SIOUX CITY GAS LIGHT CO.'S WORKS.

To illustrate its importance and immensity, attention need only be called to the fact that, just west of the Missouri River, after it again turns north, at a point over 100 miles west of Sioux City, lies the great Sioux Indian Reservation, a splendid agricultural and grazing region, of which 16,000 square miles—an area of incomparably richer natural resources than any one of a dozen States of the Union, which might be mentioned—has just been opened by Congress to settlement. The drainage of this region flows almost due east into the Missouri, and along the valleys of these tributary streams, two great corporations—the Chicago, Milwaukee & St. Paul, and the Chicago & Northwestern—are hastening to build lines into the wonderful mineral and cattle regions beyond, carrying the fruits of the same over their main systems to Sioux City; and, on the other hand, from it as the distributing point supplying them and the thousands of settlers who will flock into that territory.

But the significant fact is that so vast a country as this Sioux reservation, now newly opened to development, is only a fraction of Sioux City's trade territory, bound up in a common interest with it alike by the artificial systems of communication and the physical outlines and conformation of the country. This is why there is a city where Sioux City is.

In the early day, settlement of the Northwest followed the water courses, and the trade supply thereof went by the water routes. Consequently Sioux City was the natural and necessary depot for the upper Missouri valley; for the Missouri is navigable 1,900 miles above Sioux City. And precisely so, too, when railroads were pushed into the Northwest, the converging point, according to the indications of the grades of the streams, was at Sioux City. It is interesting to note, in this connection, that the first railroad to reach Sioux City, the Sioux City & Pacific, was diverted from a projected west line across Nebraska to a junction with the Union Pacific, to its present line south to Council Bluffs, because of the absence of

CHICAGO, MILWAUKEE & ST. PAUL PASSENGER DEPOT.

engineering difficulties along the Missouri valley. So, too, the railroad systems which have since gridironed the Northwest have followed the valleys of these streams which converge at Sioux City.

Here, then, is a tributary territory, opening westwardly and northwestwardly from Sioux City which it is no exaggeration to term an empire. To be identified with its expanding development is to be a great city, and the fact of such connection explains the growth of Sioux City. For, be it remembered, within all this realm Sioux City has not even a single rival. Chicago is distant 544 miles to the east; Minneapolis and St. Paul 270 miles northeast, and Omaha over 100 miles due south. It was not till after 1880 that the flood of immigration began to pour into this territory, and since then over 500,000 settlers have been added to Dakota, and 200,000 to Northern Nebraska, and 100,000 to fifteen counties around Sioux City in Northwestern Iowa. And this has been the period of Sioux City's growth: railroads have been extended, towns and villages sprung up and the prairie turned into improved farms.

It is necessary now to consider a fact which, resting on the fundamental relation to the upper Missouri valley, is the key-stone of the arch of Sioux City's prosperity—its relation to the corn region of the Northwest and the mutual relations between the corn and range regions of the Northwest.

What, among immediate causes, most of all has made Sioux City great? The soil of the region just about it. What in the soil? Those properties which make it the greatest corn section, not only in the United States, but also in the world. Take the territory about Sioux City, including Northwestern Iowa, and the adjacent land in Southern Dakota and Northern Nebraska within a radius of 100 miles, extending indefinitely upwards along the flood plains of the Missouri River and its tributaries, and the United States may be challenged for another region equalling or approaching this as a corn country. It is not to be understood because stress is laid upon this region as a corn country, as the best corn country which

CHICAGO, ST. PAUL MINNEAPOLIS & OMAHA SHOPS.

the sun shines on, that it is not also, and for the same reasons which make it a corn country, surpassingly fruitful in all the substantial cereals and other agricultural products.

This is the pre-eminent corn country of the continent, because it has never had, from any cause, a failure of corn. Drought and excessive moisture do not disastrously affect it, as they do the corn fields of Eastern Iowa, Illinois, and sections adjacent thereto. The latter, indeed, are splendid producers of corn, but successful years in that crop alternate with failures. The crowning felicity of the Sioux City corn field, the pre-eminent excellence of the Northwestern soil, is not merely its extraordinary fertility, but also its average availability for agricultural purposes, year after year. Thus, while in 1887, a year of disastrous failure of corn in Eastern Iowa and Illinois, there was, in Nebraska, not many miles from Sioux City, a field growing 85 bushels of corn to the acre, the same being the twenty-sixth successive corn crop on the same field, there has not been known, in thirty years, a single failure of the corn crop in the Northwestern region. Moreover, the peculiar character of the soil of the Northwestern corn field makes it much more easy and far less expensive to cultivate - to plow, to plant, to tend the crop.

3

All these facts appear as well from scientific examination of these soils as from practical experience; and an adequate study of them clears away the mystery, how the people, now partially occupying them, have been able to accumulate, in ten or fifteen years, as much wealth as it required twenty-five or fifty years to accumulate in other portions of the West which are themselves regarded as extraordinarily fertile and which really are so. Professor Charles A. White, now of Smithsonian Institution at Washington,

PEAVEY BROS., WHOLESALE HARDWARE.

D. C., made an exhaustive survey of these soils, publishing the results of his explorations in two large volumes which are regarded as standard authority in the scientific world on both sides of the Ocean.

The soils of the corn district of the northwest, as described above, are three in number, the drift, the "bluff," or loess, as the Germans call a similar soil in the famous valley of the Rhine, and the alluvial. The drift covers the larger portion of the area described, the undulating prairie being an example. It covers the earth like a mantle, hiding the stratified rocks from view. It forms both the soil and the sub-soil, the average depth in Northwestern Iowa being 200 feet and rarely falling as low as 100 feet. It is one profound mass of rich soil. Two all-important consequences follow. In the first place, there are, near the surface, no indurated clay or rock strata to act as a bowl, retaining excessive moisture. In short, the surface drift is naturally underdrained, so that superabundant rainfall, which would cause total fail-ure of crops on the thinner drift of other parts of Iowa and the west, has never produced such a result in Northwestern Iowa since its original settlement. And, in the second place, on account of precisely the

FIRST NATIONAL BANK.

same conditions, no other soil can so resist the evil effects of drought. The vast depth of fine, friable drift, acts as a sponge to retain meager moisture, whereas a thin soil, however rich, resting on a hard stra-tum, would speedily become impoverished of water. No matter how severe the drought may be, the drift soil of the Northwest holds within itself an inexhaustible reservoir of moisture, to be brought to the sur-face by evaporation or tapped by the roots of growing crops, which, in time of drought, strike deeper in quest of water.

Of the two other soils, the "bluff" deposit is the more remarkable, as well as the greater in extent. The bluffs along the Missouri River are formed of this soil, which is deposited in a vast layer over the more common drift, to an average distance of twenty-five miles on each side of the river and to a maximum depth of 200 feet. As in the drift so in the "bluff," there are no stratified rocks, and not even a boulder. The bluff soil is, in fact, the sediment dropped in the marshes, marking the lowest level of a great lake, which was, later, drained by the Missouri River ages before the country assumed its present physical aspect. The bluff soil, therefore, is even more fertile than the drift, into which, at its outer edges, it grades imperceptibly, having like it, also, perfect underdrainage.

The last division comprises the soils of the alluvial flood plains of the river valleys, or, as they are popularly called, "bottom lands." The importance of these soils readily appears from the fact that Northwestern Iowa is covered with an intricate network of rivers and minor tributaries; and what is true of Northwestern Iowa in this respect, is also true of Southeastern Dakota and Northeastern Nebraska.

A. M. HALEY & SON'S MACHINE SHOPS.

These soils are, as an eminent scientific authority puts it, "the most fertile in the state," from the fact that they contain the washings of the other soils in addition to a large amount of decayed vegetable matter, derived through the agency of former floods from the luxuriant growth along the borders of the streams.

Such are the three grand divisions of marvelous soil—the drift, the "bluff," and the alluvial—all further enriched near the surface by a generous admixture of decayed vegetable and animal matter, which renders Northwestern Iowa, and in kindred manner also adjacent portions of Dakota and Nebraska, a region absolutely unrivaled in the whole United States for agricultural production. It yields all the great staple products—corn, wheat, oats, rye, flax, grass, and root crops, etc.—in amount and regularity of return nowhere else even approached. Corn is King. Here, neither excessive rainfall nor drought has ever, or can ever cause failure of crops, and the yield, whether in point of luxuriance or of fineness of quality, knows no rival in the markets of the world. And this cream of the cream of the corn lands of the United

States is the very life of the cattle and hog interests, which, within the short period since the beginning of cultivation in this region, have grown to such enormous proportions. Thrift and prosperity are the children of such abounding goodness of nature. Their many handed proofs are scattered in the improved farms, the multiplying villages, and towns, and cities, all the scenes of fruitful enterprise, and

IOWA SAVINGS BANK.

all the results of industry during comparatively only a few years. In the very heart of all, at the point of convergence of the drainage of all this region, as reference to the map shows, is Sioux City, not only the geographical, but also the undisputed commercial center, its arteries of trade radiating in every direction and following, of necessity, the natural water routes, and bound together by the very logic of the situation. The cause of the growth of Sioux City is no mystery. It has grown because it must grow—because of

SIOUX CITY ILLUSTRATED.

the mutual relations subsisting between it and the marvellous richness of the soils of its immediate
agricultural environment, because Corn is King, and because his capital and throne are at Sioux City.

METROPOLITAN BLOCK—ERECTED AND OWNED BY S. DESPARDIS.

But to appreciate the forces which are pushing Sioux City forward, the eye must glance beyond the
splendid cornfield immediately around about it. That, indeed, by itself, is sufficient when fully

developed, to maintain a great city—a city many times even the Sioux City of to-day. For the twenty counties of Northwestern Iowa, which are within the assured range of Sioux City's trade, are less than one-third of the northwestern corn region, which includes as well the adjacent portions of Southeastern Dakota and Northeastern Nebraska, lying on both sides of the Missouri River, westward of Sioux City. The northern edge of the corn belt is only a few tiers of counties north, and thence its boundary curves around Sioux City southwesterly in Dakota and Nebraska. This is the great body of the distinctively corn country, and although the boundary line is not regular, it is located at no great distance, relatively speaking, west and northwest from Sioux City, except along river valleys, which, of course, extend it in narrow strips considerably beyond the general western limit. Sioux City, thus, is in the

SIOUX CITY SAVINGS BANK, (RICHARDSON BLOCK.)

corner of the northwestern corn country, while the rich corn fields are carried indefinitely east and south across the State of Iowa.

Beyond this limit to the west and north, corn, as the main crop, cannot be profitably raised. Now, fix in the mind the vast stretches of prairie across Western Nebraska and Dakota, through the foot-hills of the Black Hills into the mountain country itself, and into the broken surfaces of Wyoming and Montana. Note that these vast ranges open upon the great northwestern angle of the corn country, in which Sioux City is located, the Missouri Valley sweeping from the west and the northwest and draining them before it receives at Sioux City the combined drainage of the corn country. Note, likewise, that Sioux City is not only the natural entrepot to the corn country from the range country, and therefore, conversely, to the latter from the former, but also that it is in the most direct line for transporting cattle from the ranges to eastern and ultimate markets; and, furthermore, that the lines of railroad transportation, taking direction from the natural drainage of the country, connect the ranges, across Western Nebraska and Dakota, with Sioux City, and thence in every direction run through its surrounding corn country, as well as communicating with Chicago and the East.

These are business of a corn country and of a corn country, they are a grass country. Soon after the war, cattle in immense numbers began to be driven north from Texas to the northwestern ranges, and

JOY & MARKS' BLOCK.

for twelve or fifteen years, so luxuriant was the natural growth of bunch grass in Montana and Wyoming and the buffalo grass of Western Dakota, that they could be fattened and made ready to go directly to market. The profits were fabulous. Cattle companies, multiplying everywhere in this and foreign lands, covered the ranges with hundreds of thousands of cattle. The result was an over-stocking of the ranges. The grass was eaten off. Settlers, too, came in, cutting off free access to water courses. A revolution in range methods was wrought. The cattle could no longer be fattened on native grass. In that condition winter storms decimated them.

The pressure of these conditions began to be severely felt as early as 1882, and it has increased with each succeeding year. Cattle could still be grown and their frames built on the ranges—grown and built there, indeed, more cheaply than elsewhere—but the profit was all in fat cattle. The inexorable logic of the situation, accordingly, was that the cattle must be moved from the ranges to be fattened; they must be transferred to where corn is grown. The corn was just at hand; it was to be found in the Corn Region, in the northwestern corner of which Sioux City is situated. This region was in the direct line of transit to Chicago, so that cattle could be taken from the ranges to Sioux City, to be distributed thence among the

farmers of the corn country for fattening, and then re-shipped to Chicago.

Beginning in 1882 the stream of cattle, flowing through Sioux City for distribution thence in smaller bunches for fattening at the corn-cribs of the northwest, has rapidly increased. It has now

HOTEL GARRETSON—OWNED AND CONDUCTED BY D. A. WILLIAMS.

swelled to enormous proportions. Not only so, but there is a counter current of young stock and stock cattle of all kinds, flowing out from the farms of the corn country, through Sioux City to the ranges, which are the great breeding country. The ranchmen have learned that, although the great herd must go, they may by improved methods, in future breed and raise in the aggregate even more cattle than in the past. And so the stream of cattle from the ranges to the corn region, through Sioux City as a gateway, has grown larger each succeeding year since 1882, and in the nature of things must in future grow still larger, until the mutual possibilities of the two great sections are fulfilled. But these are boundless—practically boundless.

The multiplication of transactions involved in distributing cattle through the northwestern country, as early as 1884 and 1885, had made Sioux City an important stock market. When it was once finally established that a large portion of the immense herds of the ranges must be brought to the corn region, another not less vital fact was also thereby established, although it may not, at first, have been so generally and so clearly perceived, to-wit, that the cattle must eventually be slaughtered at Sioux City. For, as is universally conceded now, as there was great profit in bringing the range cattle for distribution through the corn country for fattening, there is, for the same reason, still greater economy in slaughtering and dressing the beeves before shipping them on to Chicago, or to final market.

Moreover, the northwest was not only a vast corn field, but it was an enormous hog-pen. Being a cattle country because it was a corn country, it was, therefore, also a great hog country. The steer and the

RESIDENCE JAMES G. MILLER.

hog go together, and both together form the close fitting halves of a machine for working up and condensing the raw material of the corn-field.

Moved thereto by the multiplying transactions in cattle and hogs, leading men in Sioux City in 1884 organized the Union Stock Yards Company, which is properly enumerated above as one of the important instruments of the growth of the city. The facilities thus afforded were the first formal outreachings towards making Sioux City the dominant market city which it now is; and in their immediate vicinity, and operating in harmony therewith, are the great packing establishments since located here.

Sioux City, indeed, had had for many years an important packing interest, one extensive packing house; but, although highly important to Sioux City, this did not make the town a packing center, a recognized and dominant stock market in the whole territory of its trade. This was the situation in the

THE HORNICK DRUG CO.

early part of 1887, when there occurred the seemingly sudden movement of the great Chicago packers of beef and pork to Sioux City, and to the establishment here of packing houses, which have beyond peradventure settled it that Sioux City is, and is to remain, the stock market and packing center of the Northwest; and this has been confirmed by the actual construction, within less than a year, of the immense packing houses of Silberhorn and of Fowler, of Chicago, recognized the world over as kings of the meat interest. And in addition to the great Booge packing house previously long established, there is virtual certainty of construction here also of a mammoth dressed beef establishment by Swift of Chicago. But, to say nothing of what is to be added immediately, the packing houses already in actual operation, having capacity for 15,000 hogs and 2,000 cattle daily, constitute a vast meat industry, and have raised Sioux City, at one stroke, to the front rank as a hog and cattle market in the United States. And by this

RESIDENCE C. F. HOYT.

capital achievement there is involved for Sioux City a great system of collateral manufactures, such as glue-works, tanning, soap-works, fertilizing works, tanneries, cooper-works, etc., etc., which are, indeed, already being supplied, affording, with the packing houses, employment for thousands of workingmen and in manifold ways building up and extending the commerce and industry of the city.

It should not be forgotten, however, that other causes were at work to produce this grand result — causes of far-reaching force, and kindred to the fundamental movements which have marked Sioux City as the capital of a great empire of trade and production in the Northwest. During the years following 1880, the fertility of the soil of the Sioux City corn region, as well as the fine farming country about it, and the adaptability of the ranges further west to stock-raising in connection with the corn country — all these and similar facts were becoming better known to the world. Immigration, having previously been temporarily diverted to other portions of the West by the seductions of land-grant corporations, then began to pour into the richer lands of the Upper Missouri Valley. The Northwest was becoming by inherent strength an independent trade empire. The obstacle of sheer distance was protection for Sioux City against the monopolizing power of Chicago, which overshadowed the less fortunate cities along the Mississippi valley south of Minneapolis and St. Paul.

The salient fact of the independent force of the Upper Missouri Valley was recognized by the great railroad corporations which pierced the northwest from Chicago, and which had been disposed by self-interest, or supposed self-interest, to be the instruments of the trade monopoly of Chicago and by

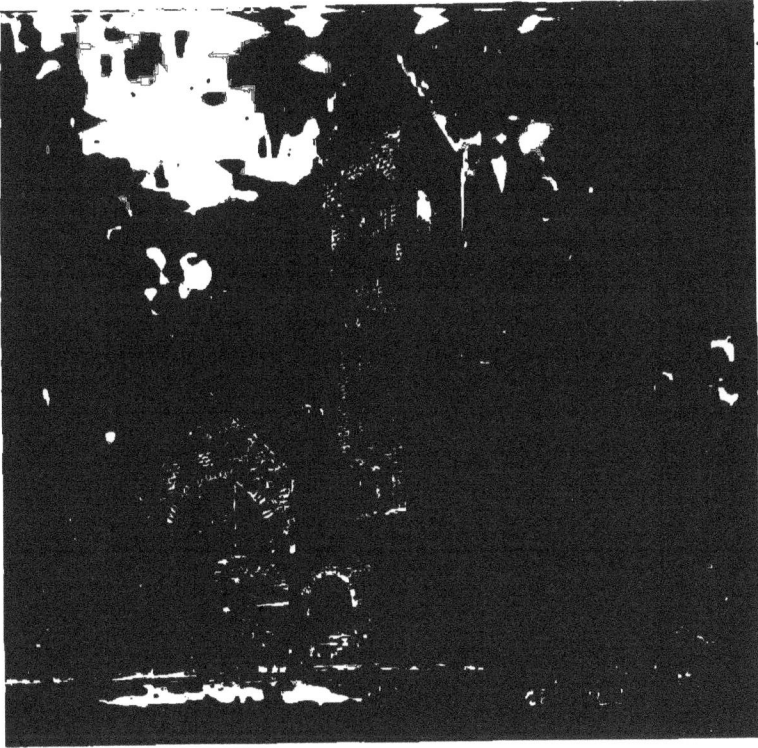

THE FIRST CONGREGATIONAL CHURCH.

discriminating rates to girdle the growth of minor western trade centers. It was upon this enforced change of policy on the part of the corporations, about 1886, toward Missouri river market cities, Kansas City, Omaha and Sioux City, that the movement of the Chicago packers thereto was predicated.

If there were space, it would be interesting to pause here and consider in detail the building of railroads in the Upper Missouri Valley, and their centralization at Sioux City. The extraordinary and absolutely unparalleled development of this vast region, with whose growth and destiny the growth of Sioux City is indissolubly bound up, has been conditioned upon the building of railroads, as well as upon the marvelous richness of its soil; for by the former the fruits of the latter are made available, and the rapid tendency to lower rates of transportation, especially during the past ten years, has had the effect to bring the cheap rich lands of the northwest practically as near the seaboard markets as the high-priced and exhausted lands of the east.

If the reader will refer to an accurate map of that portion of the Upper Missouri Valley, comprising Northwestern Iowa, Southwestern Minnesota, Northern Nebraska, Southern Dakota, and the eastern portions of Wyoming and Montana, he will observe the centralization of the railroad communications at Sioux City. Such centralization is the logical and necessary result of the convergence precisely at Sioux City of the natural drainage of this region, to which reference has already been made. The lines of railroad, following of necessity the river valleys, converged upon Sioux City, and from it reached the great empire immediately westward and northwestward along the Upper Missouri Valley.

Thus Sioux City is the point of convergence of five great railroad systems, viz: the Illinois Central, the Chicago & Northwestern, the Chicago, Milwaukee & St. Paul, the Chicago, St. Paul, Minneapolis

RESIDENCE CRAIG L. WRIGHT.

& Omaha, and, including the Sioux City & Northern, on which construction is just beginning, the "Manitoba" system. The Sioux City & Pacific, the first road to reach Sioux City in 1868, is now a part of the Chicago & Northwestern system. The process of centralization of the railroad communications of the northwest not only has made Sioux City the converging point of the main lines of these five great systems, but has brought hither, as any railroad map shows, thirteen branch lines, nearly all located according to the convenience of the grades of river valleys and their tributaries.

Sioux City is the western terminus of the Illinois Central, which last year acquired ownership of the lines running eastward across Iowa, long operated by it under lease, while two new branch lines have been built within the year, the one northwest into Dakota, and the other southwest, opening up to the trade of Sioux City a large new territory. Two great railroad systems, the Chicago, Milwaukee & St. Paul, and the Chicago & Northwestern have reached out giant arms from Sioux City westwardly and northwestwardly across Southern Dakota, spider-webbing that immense territory in every direction with feeders. These systems, with present Dakota termini on the Missouri river, but preparing and ready to push on into and across the great Sioux Indian Reservation, are the handmaids of the trade of Sioux City therein, making it as well the market of this empire as its depot of supply.

THE SIOUX CITY HIGH SCHOOL.

Not less intimately is Northern Nebraska, lying directly west of Sioux City on the opposite shore of the Missouri River, bound up in commercial interest with Sioux City. The main line of the Chicago, St. Paul, Minneapolis & Omaha reaches Sioux City by the valley of the Floyd river, which joins the

Missouri within the corporate limits of the city, and from the opposite shore pierces Northern Nebraska with three lines. Pending completion of the railroad bridge across the river, connection between the two shores is effected, as it has been for many years, by a temporary bridge during the winter season and by steamboat transfer during the summer. The machine shops of this company are located here as are those also of the Chicago, Milwaukee & St. Paul.

During the past few years the Chicago & Northwestern, having covered Southern Dakota, has made an equally bold movement across Northern Nebraska. Crossing the Missouri River by a bridge seventy-five miles below Sioux City, and acquiring the Fremont, Elkhorn & Missouri Valley line, the great Chicago & Northwestern has not only covered Northeastern Nebraska up to the shore opposite Sioux City, but also boldly pushed its main line westwardly along the line of the Niobrara into the Black Hills

RESIDENCE T. J. STONE.

and into the regions beyond. This bold extension has tapped, from the south, at once the great cattle country and the resourceful mineral districts of the Black Hills.

Such was the situation at the beginning of 1886, and during that year the importance of Sioux City was recognized by the great railroad corporations by building to it numerous connecting lines necessary to their systems. At the close of 1886, the great desideratum, the one missing link which the expanding necessities of the situation could no longer leave unsupplied, was a railroad bridge across the Missouri River. The time was ripe, and in the early spring of 1887, the Chicago & Northwestern and the Chicago, St. Paul, Minneapolis & Omaha Companies made stipulations for spanning the river with the splendid structure now nearing completion, using therefor the charter secured by Sioux City years before. With the bridge, the railroad problem, in its potency has been finally solved, and the last barrier to the complete commercial supremacy of Sioux City in Northern Nebraska has been overleaped and forever removed.

Such a system of railroads, radiating from Sioux City through a magnificent territory in the north-west, one hundred and fifty miles north and south and over six hundred miles east and west, including Northern Nebraska and Southern Dakota, from Sioux City to the Black Hills, in addition to the whole northwestern quarter of the State of Iowa—such a system involves exclusive transportation facilities for Sioux City, which compel it to be a great trade center. Sioux City, indeed, from its foundation has been a jobbing center. Before a railroad had been built into the northwest, or had even reached Sioux City,

BANKING ROOM, DIRECTORS' ROOM   SECURITY NATIONAL BANK.

the depot of supplies to such settlements as had then been made further west and to the government stations and trading posts was established here, the means of transportation being the steamboat and the freighter's wagon.

The substitution of the railroad for the older methods of transportation in the northwest, the remarkable movement of railroad construction during recent years to cover the specific region of Sioux City's environment, has simply afforded means for the more rapid development of its jobbing trade. Description of the jobbing interests of Sioux City need not go into detail; they are the logical counterpart of the great system of railroads which is their instrument and servant. The jobbing interests represent all the leading lines of supply and respond to the necessities of the people of the great territory in the northwest reached from Sioux City. The cuts and illustrations given in these pages fairly represent some of the leading jobbing houses, and from them, as well as from the suggestions of the relation of Sioux City to the Upper Missouri Valley, may be inferred the strength of the jobbing business better than from rehearsal of figures and dry statistics.

Rapid as has been the growth of the jobbing interest during the past five years, it has been a constant struggle for the Sioux City jobbers to keep pace with the demands of the tributary territory, to increase their capital and other facilities to correspond with its development. Every one of the tens of thousands of settlers who have annually for ten years last past gone into this territory, every town and

RESIDENCE H. A. JANDT.

village which has sprung up therein, every mile of railroad built, as the march of development has been moving step by step westward each and all these things have been drafts upon the resources of Sioux City as the jobbing center of this territory. And if there be adequate conception of the tremendous development of the Upper Missouri Valley during this period, it will be understood why the jobbing interest of Sioux City has grown so rapidly, and why, notwithstanding the profits thereof have been re-invested from year to year, and new houses added and all facilities constantly enlarged, the jobbers of Sioux City are to-day taxed to the extreme limit of their resources to meet the demands upon them.

The possibilities of Sioux City for trade are forcibly suggested by the fact that of the empire about it, which has already made of it a jobbing center, less than 25 per cent. is as yet occupied and developed. And into this territory immigration is pouring a constantly rising stream. The new settlers represent the most enterprising, intelligent and prosperous elements of the States north of the Ohio River, from which, mainly, they come. And the process of development upon the surpassingly rich bottom lands and prairies of the Upper Missouri Valley, in this day of railroads and improved agricultural agencies, is incomparably more rapid than it was in the pioneer days of Ohio, Indiana and Illinois, when the settler must literally hew his way into the wilderness and fight the long hard battle in absolute isolation.

When population in the Upper Missouri Valley shall double, treble and quadruple, as it infallibly will during the next decade, it is apparent that the trade of Sioux City therein will more than double, treble and quadruple, just as during the past decade there has been such notable expansion of the facilities of supply here in exact correspondence with the increasing demands of the tributary territory. For absolute certainty has now taken the place of uncertainty; the lines of communication have now become finally fixed; a great jobbing interest has been firmly established and built up; nothing remains

JANDT & TOMPKINS, WHOLESALE DRY GOODS AND NOTIONS.

but steady, logical and assured growth upon the broad foundation already laid and toward the destiny which the obvious conditions of the situation have marked out.

Taking under one sweep of the eye the magnificent territory of the Upper Missouri Valley, opening about and above Sioux City, consider now that it is in the most direct natural route from Chicago and the lake region to the Pacific. At least two of Sioux City's great railroad systems are not only tapping in every direction and bearing to it the wealth of a great empire in the northwest, but are rapidly reaching westward for transcontinental connections. The certainty of the near future must be the counter extension of the Central Pacific eastward, and the logic of the conditions compels such extension by way of Sioux City; while, on the other hand, the "Manitoba" system is reaching from a port on Lake Superior, independent of Chicago, a hand already almost to Sioux City, and a tax already voted, and construction just ready to begin, will during the present summer clasp this extended hand.

Such are only a few of the broad indications, only a few of the accomplished facts, of the situation of the Sioux City of To-day. Elaboration of detail could hardly emphasize its manifest destiny—could not more clearly reveal its fixed relation of market and supply city to the Upper Missouri Valley.

In the foregoing brief and imperfect survey it has been the purpose to present, in their broad phases, the distinctive relations of Sioux City and its tributary territory, rather than to enlarge descriptively on the numerous features in detail which, as a rule, are common to all towns and cities of equal size; it has likewise been the purpose to state, without coloring or exaggeration, the facts as they actually exist, and in all cases where there was doubt in regard to estimates, to lean to the conservative side, so that all who may be interested to make further inquiry into the specific facts of the actual status and common

RESIDENCE ED. HAAKINSON.

destiny of Sioux City and the Upper Missouri Valley, will find that the splendid truth, far from being fully told, has only been partially suggested in these pages.

One thing more must be referred to, viz.: the agency of Sioux City itself in realizing upon the natural advantages of its position as already outlined. Sioux City has not waited in the first instance for the outside world to see the inherent relations subsisting between it and the Upper Missouri Valley. Had the men of Sioux City pursued a passive policy, relying solely on the natural advantages of the situation, obvious and commanding though they are, to build a city here, the transition from a frontier post to a dominant trade center must have been far less rapid, to say the least, and there might possibly have been division of the magnificent territory, now assured to it forever, to other trade centers within the same.

But the men of Sioux City, from the very first, have been instant in all the great enterprises, public and private, which in their combined result have now established its commercial primacy in the Upper Missouri Valley according to the natural indications of the same. Throughout the entire series of achievements tending to this end Sioux City itself has taken the initiative, and, acting on the faith which it had in itself,

SIOUX CITY ILLUSTRATED.

has established itself in the faith of the world, thereby bringing in the co-operation of the capital and enterprise of the east, and enlisting the aid of the great railroad corporations and other concerns which have done so much for Sioux City.

There is not, and never has been, division of counsel, faction or jealousy in Sioux City, but in the presence of opportunity for public enterprise all citizens of all classes have fused in enthusiastic harmony, whether the proposition was a tax in aid of a railroad, to build a bridge, to insure machine shops, or any other important work. It is this public-spirited harmony, under the direction of the far-seeing and intrepid leadership of a few prominent citizens—men who have themselves voluntarily assumed great burdens and risks in the common cause—it is thus that Sioux City may be said at least to have accelerated the destiny which its natural relation to the Upper Missouri Valley marked out for it. By such in-

HAAKINSON BLOCK.

dependent endeavor nearly every trunk line of railroad, and most of the branch lines, now converging here were secured; thus the opera house; thus the great hotel; thus the first of the machine shops; thus many of the important commercial and manufacturing interests. But the most notable fruits of this policy have been within the period of eighteen months last past, during which were secured those capital achievements, the railroad bridge across the Missouri, the great packing establishments, three new branch lines of railroad and assurance of a new trunk line, as well as the wonderful Corn Palace.

And the same spirit of public enterprise, strengthened and emboldened by the results of the past, and engaged with the greater enterprises now in hand and in immediate prospect, is to-day, next to the natural advantages of its position, the most notable feature of the situation of Sioux City. And thus has come to pass the confidence which Sioux City has in itself, and which the world has now come to have in it, so that there is nothing within the splendid possibilities of the Upper Missouri Valley which it cannot accomplish.

THE CORN PALACE.

THE NEW WONDER OF THE WORLD.

"In the land of the Ojibways,
In the pleasant land and peaceful,
Sing the mysteries of Mondamin,
Sing the blessings of the corn-fields."

Longfellow.

PROPOSED RESIDENCE JAS. A. JACKSON, (MORNING SIDE.)

The Sioux City Corn Palace was unquestionably the most beautiful and novel, as well as the most appropriate, edifice ever erected in this country for the exclusive purpose of displaying agricultural products. It was unique. Nothing of the kind was ever before seen. President Cleveland declared: "This is the first new thing that has been shown me." Mr. Chauncey M. Depew said: "I have been all over the world, nearly, but I never before saw a Corn Palace." Travelers, whose eyes had rested upon the famous works of mankind in all portions of the globe, expressed the greatest admiration for this creation of western genius wrought from the products of western soil. It was an artistic triumph, marking the beginning of a new era in expositions of its class, an absolutely new idea the appropriateness of which evoked not only the enthusiasm of the people of Sioux City and the Upper Missouri Valley, the fruits of whose toil and the felicity of whose fortune it so vividly typified, but also the interest of the people of all sections of the country.

This record of the great event is prepared that those persons who did not see the Corn Palace of 1887 may, from reading an impartial narrative of the incidents of the Festival and a description of the building, form an estimate of the character and interest of the occasion; and, more than this, gain some idea of the industrial and productive forces of the richly dowered region of which the Sioux City Corn Palace, as well as Sioux City itself, is so striking a suggestion.

The idea of constructing a Corn Palace was original with Sioux City. The carrying out of that idea, to a degree far beyond the anticipations of its originators and to the eminent satisfaction of the one hundred and forty thousand visitors who beheld its consummation, was the work of Sioux City men. A Sioux City architect designed the plan and Sioux City artisans executed it. Sioux City women adorned the interior of the structure. Therefore it may be reasonably claimed that, as St. Paul has its Ice Palace, St. Louis its Veiled Prophets, and New Orleans its Mardi Gras, so the metropolis of the Upper Missouri region has the sole right to the Corn Palace. And thus, having presented something new under the sun, the

ST. CROIX LUMBER CO.

triumphant materialization of an original thought, Sioux City may with propriety proclaim itself to be the "Corn Palace City of the World."

While the completed Corn Palace embodied an original idea of satisfying and comprehensive significance, it is not to be understood that there was at the start definite and complete consciousness of the idea. It rather grew with the making of the Corn Palace. The decorative possibilities of the corn plant and of the other products of the Sioux City corn-field, far from being understood at the outset, were not even dreamed of. But the people of Sioux City, with the remarkable growth of their city as the prominent fact in mind, had the keenest appreciation of the productive energies of the soil of the northwestern empire about them. The fundamental fact, upon which rested the prosperity of Sioux City, its great and suddenly developing packing interests, the concentration here of the business exchanges, the trade and the communications of the Upper Missouri Valley, was the prosperity of this region as an agricultural region, and the mainstay of the latter was Corn— King Corn. Some account of the fertility of this region, and of the mutual relations subsisting between it and Sioux City as its geographical and commercial center, has been given in a former chapter of this work, and that account will suggest to the reader how impossible it is to understand the significance of those relations, to say nothing of experiencing it in practical dealings, without being impressed with the majesty of the king of crops in the northwest. And this was the basis on which the Corn Palace of 1887 was built at Sioux City—an enterprise to which the interest, enthusiasm and pride not only of Sioux City, but as well of the thousands on the farms and in the villages and towns of the Corn Region of the northwest, who shared in its prosperity, responded with a common impulse. The working out of the details of the Corn Palace itself, the discovery of the artistic possibilities of the corn plant, and the sudden inspiration which was born of such discovery, were things which came later—came in the work of building. As Aphrodite sprung from the ocean's foam, so, when the effort was once begun to represent the beneficence of the typical product of the northwestern field, dawned the realization of its artistic resources.

RESIDENCE FRED EVANS, JR.

An abundant harvest was ripening in this royal domain when some one in Sioux City suggested the idea of the holding of a Harvest Festival and Corn Jubilee in honor and recognition of the bounteous gift. That hint, vague and undefined though it was, sufficed to stir the spirit of enterprise in Sioux City breasts. It was the virile germ of a grand event. Then followed a more deliberate and practical consideration of the scheme.

A committee of Sioux City business men was designated to take the matter in charge and effect an operative organization. When a committee is appointed in Sioux City, it may be remarked, a foregone conclusion is that something is going to be done. Such an appointment, even by an informal body like the early Festival meetings, is not a mere honorary distinction, to be treated lightly or ignored altogether by the appointee. It is a business transaction, and exact duty is required of all. This fact is alluded to as a characteristic of Sioux City.

Another distinguishing trait of the citizens of Sioux City is the merging of the individual into the municipal whole when credit or profit is accorded by the public. In the present instance, the distinction of originating the Corn Palace is accorded to "the people." In fact, this concession is not ill-advised, because no plan was adopted and rigidly adhered to, either in the construction of the Palace or the entertainment of visitors. Hundreds of willing workers contributed gratuitously to the adornment of Palace and city, insuring success. The personal element—individual aggrandizement and commercial advertisement—was excluded from the building. The Festival was conducted, within the Palace, solely for the enhancement of agricultural interests throughout the northwest, and in the street-parades strictly to display evidences of the progress of Sioux City in commercial lines, because of the agricultural development of the region.

The opportunity for a noble effort and the men capable of noble performance came face to face—a country weighted with ripening grain; a city filled with alert intelligence and executive force. A combination of such circumstantial power is invincible as fate.

Among the first propositions regarding decorations was one that the Woodbury County courthouse be trimmed with corn and used as a hall; another suggestion was to heap great piles of corn along the streets; and finally some one suggested that a "Corn

W. E. HIGMAN & CO., WHOLESALE BOOTS AND SHOES.

Palace" be erected.

An architect submitted a plan for a special building, 60 by 60 feet in size, closely resembling the main structure as subsequently erected. This design was discussed and amended so as to contemplate the construction of a palace 100 by 100 feet in ground dimensions. Drawings were made in detail by the architect and unanimously adopted. Committees on finance and programme, consisting of leading citizens, were appointed, and the contract was awarded for constructing the frame of the building. Later,

as the magnitude and significance of the enterprise were perceived, the Sioux City Corn Palace Association was formed, and the work sub-divided among a number of committees.

Vacant lots on the northwest corner of Fifth and Jackson streets were selected as the site of the Palace. Here was a clear frontage of 100 feet on Fifth street. Immediately to the west was a high one-story wooden building, 50 feet on Fifth street by 150 feet deep, which was designed for a roller-skating rink and contained a smooth, solid floor.

Work was at once begun. A crude but strong frame was set up and sheeted with rough lumber. At the center rose a well-proportioned square tower, 100 feet in height, with massive cupola having arched windows, and corner minarets, and terminating in a four-sided pinnacle and flag-staff. At each of the corners of the building was a square tower, 20 by 20 feet in size, with lofty four-sided apex roof and minarets. Midway of the Fifth street and Jackson street fronts were square towers, with flat roofs and minarets. Springing from the inmost corners of the exterior towers to the outward corners of the main tower, on a line with the base of the apex of each, were light festoons, or, to use the architectural term, flying buttresses, which imparted an effect of massiveness to the edifice. The roof-lines were harmoniously irregular, sweeping from the central tower to the exterior as the several front elevations required. This broken outline was intentional, in order that a maximum of surface might be presented for decoration. The apertures in the towers were spacious, generally of an arched style along the upper courses and the main entrances, but angular in the ground-course of the corner towers. This purpose was also to give variety of outline, for the better display of decorative materials. Thus, while the

RESIDENCE F. R. KIRK.

structure was of a composite and an original architectural order, the plan was admirably adapted to the uses for which it was designed.

As work upon the Corn Palace progressed, the managers became more and more conscious of the possibilities in decoration. They did not at first conceive that it would be an affair of extraordinary magnitude nor an object of surpassing beauty. Probably the projectors had given but little or no thought to the artistic phase of the subject when that additional pledge of success stood revealed by accident before them. The originators' minds were bent upon the practical consideration of the value of corn as a staple and of hogs as a profitable medium of trade. Their idea was to impress the public with indisputable evidence of the productiveness of this region. But the people asserted such an interest in the celebration, each individual suggesting an improvement or an elaboration of the plan, that the palace and the festival at large soon passed beyond the original plans and became everybody's work. The citizens went corn crazy. The city itself was inundated in a flood of corn. And so the development of the Corn Palace, from an arch across a street or a few meager decorations on some building already standing, to the magnificent temple in which Ceres might have felt honored to abide, was the natural outgrowth of favorable circumstances, not a deliberately preconceived idea strictly adhered to. Like the corn, it sprang from an insignificant germ to thrive and bloom and mature under the fervid heat of congenial

PEAVEY & STEPHENS, WHOLESALE AND RETAIL FURNITURE.

conditions. It was a popular work, and therefore proved, from very spontaneity, its power to reach the hearts of its beholders. It was the personification of Art in Nature. The humblest blade of grass was given a value; the homeliest form was made to bear its share in bringing something to the light. Thus, the practical put on the garb of the beautiful and the commercial project of a Corn Festival culminated in a feast of the Esthetic.

The frame work was scarcely completed before the inadequacy of space was realized. To meet this unexpected requirement, the skating-rink already referred to was made an annex, and within a day or two from that time, a second addition, extending westward from the rink to the Baptist Church, and 20 feet in depth, was decided upon. This arrangement gave nearly double the space for exhibits originally planned for, besides placing a spacious and solidly-floored room at the disposal of the management.

HOTEL BOOGE, B. L. CHENEY, PROPRIETOR.

The Corn Palace was, therefore, about 210 feet in length along Fifth street, by 100 feet on Jackson street, but the unequal depth of the rink and the annex gave the entire structure an average depth of 89 feet, or 18,700 square feet of floor surface.

Before undertaking a description of the decorations, without which the Palace would have been an ungainly pile of rough materials, an idea of the magnitude of the labor and wealth expended thereon is imparted by giving some of the builder's estimates. There were 300,000 feet of lumber consumed; 15,000 bushels of yellow corn and 5,000 bushels of variegated varieties; 500 pounds of carpet tacks; 3,000 pounds of nails; 1,500 pounds of small brads; 2,500 feet of rope; 500 pounds of small wire, and 3,500 yards of cloth. It took forty-six men six days to erect the palace, and nearly 300 men and women to place the decorations in form. Ten teams were employed fifteen days hauling the corn and grains.

Two steam saws were engaged constantly eight days cutting corn-ears into small pieces for decorative signs and ornamental work. Besides this labor is all that was done by farmers in delivering grains from their own stocks. The total cost of the Palace, not including a vast amount of labor and materials gratuitously contributed, was about $28,000.

The exterior of the Corn Palace was entirely covered with corn and grains, in sheaf, stalk and ear. The many-angled roof, from the topmost point of the central tower—itself a sheaf of wheat—was thatched with grain; mainly with stalks on which the ripened ears were exposed. The festoons from central to outlying towers were draped with grains in the straw. The perpendicular surfaces of the tower and the other elevated sections were laid thickly with stalks denuded of blades and

OFFICE AND PARLOR, HOTEL BOOGE.

ears, with yellow and red ears of corn nailed firmly into fanciful patterns, and with clusters of sorghum-cane. High up on the tower, facing south and east, were huge signs bearing the words "CORN PALACE," wrought from transverse sections of corn-ears. The windows in all the towers were latticed with ears strung on wires. Some of those ears were red, others yellow, and still others white, giving that variety of coloring which was at once the charm and the novelty of the general effect.

The upright surfaces of the Fifth street and Jackson street fronts were sheathed with ears, laid on in square blocks, alternating perpendicular and horizontal, of different colors, producing a suggestion of mosaic. The windows and entrances, as well as the open spaces on the ground line of corner towers, were formed with ears, in patterns conforming to the style of the aperture. The minarets were capped with bundles of grain and covered with stalks. As there were seventy of these, the airiness of the effect can easily be imagined.

The front of the rink, or "Armory Hall," was encrusted with trimmed stalks and ears, and bore the legend, "WELCOME TO THE FIRST CORN PALACE," worked in sections of ears, and the business office signs, across its ample surface.

The unlimited use of those pieces of corn-ears in and about the palace, as well as in the private decorations of the city, calls for an explanation of what they were and how they were applied. Sound ears were sawed into sections of one and two inches in length, leaving a fringe of kernels. These pieces could then be fastened upon a sign-board or on any flat surface by a small nail driven through the pith. When different colors were combined, a very gorgeous style of block-letter was produced. Singly they looked like bright rosettes.

RESIDENCE H. A. LYON.

Above the main entrance on Fifth street was a large oil painting representing a harvest scene in the olden times. Over the entrance to the west annex was a mammoth National flag, worked in red, white and blue ears of corn. The large openings on the street were partly or wholly covered with white cloth upon which were painted typical scenes—"The Indian's Lament," cattle, hogs, etc.

Viewed from a distance of a block or two, the trifling irregularities of detail in decoration were softened and a magnificent show of color was presented to the eye. The prevailing shades were yellow; the huge structure assuming from day to day, as the sun and wind ripened the stalks, a more golden hue. The red, white and deep yellow of the corn, the brown of the sorghum and the dead green of the corn blades relieved the exterior of a monotony which might ordinarily have been expected, while the varying heights of the salient outlines added a charm of perspective, with high-lights and shadows, that combined to produce an admirable architectural effect.

The managers of the enterprise were no sooner brought face to face with the task of making the interior decorations of the place comport with the exterior than they were ready to admit their need of finer taste. The possibilities were appalling to contemplate. Time was pressing and the enormous amount of work yet to do in the space of one week was enough to create a feeling of despair. A Board of Control was appointed. An earnest invitation was issued to the women of Sioux City to lend their assistance to determine what should be done.

YOUNG MEN'S CHRISTIAN ASSOCIATION BUILDING.

Enthusiastic response greeted this appeal. A committee on decorations was formed, the interior of the main building was divided into twelve sections, and the willing workers apportioned to their several duties.

Sioux City is proud to admit that the success of the distinguished and original effort is due, in its artistic phase, to the women of Sioux City. At the beginning there were no models to work from and no coherent idea of what could be done. From bare walls, unsightly posts and a vaulting dome of ugliness was created a bower of beauty never before equalled; and yet this marvel was worked without the aid of those adjuncts of decorative art which have heretofore been deemed essential to the plans of skilled artisans. There was no gaud, no tinsel, no laying on of precious metals, no use of costly pigments. An ear of corn, a handful of grasses, a bunch of weeds, a whisp of straw—those were the materials employed. But women's deft fingers, moved by the genius, the soul, of Art, transformed such simple objects into rare and radiant loveliness.

The interior of the palace was a realm of enchantment. Under the white glare of twenty-seven electric lights, it was a vision of fairyland. The commonplace even was touched with magic wand and assumed the guise of the beautiful. The thousands of visitors who thronged through the portals on the opening night were hushed into amazed delight at the unexpected revelation before them. There was no jostling, no hurry, no confusion. The atmosphere of the place affected all alike.

RESIDENCE L. S. FAWCETT.

The strong, the delicate, the rugged, the graceful; the utilities, the harmonies; the matter-of-fact, the ethereal; all the elements in Nature's productive laboratory were here side by side, contrasting their forms in a symphony whose under-note was unity. It appealed to the cultured and the unlettered. Nature and Art were here. It was a lesson for the philosopher and the clod.

The main entrance to the palace, on the Fifth street side, was through a vaulted passage-way, without doors, but terminated by a huge screen. Upon this dark surface was wrought in cereals an effect of meadow—a study of cat-tails and grasses. Above this a large copy of the municipal seal, with a buffalo being driven from a railroad track by an engine. At right and left, on the side walls, were emblems of husbandry and a canoe, done in colored corn. On the floor stood two large stuffed hogs, with corn in mouth. Instead of proving offensive, these silent guardians of the portal served an excellent purpose, by contrast, in heightening the effect of the vision that burst upon the gaze on passing by them. The reverse of the screen was an index to the catalogue of surprises. A landscape was picked out in bits of corn-stalks, grasses and husks. A cabin, with path-way leading down, a field of grain enclosed with a fence, a family washing of corn-husk clothes hung upon a grass-blade line to dry, a well with curb and old-time sweep, a grove, and other incidental features, all laid on with regard to perspective, tone and treatment that made the picture artistically complete.

RESIDENCE CHAS. J. CLARK.

In the center of the building was an elevated platform, trimmed with mottoes of welcome done in corn. The space beneath was utilized by an exhibit of seeds put up in very attractive manner. A representation of the railroad bridge, with miniature locomotive on a popcorn track, was built of ears of corn in this compartment. High up in the tower above this stand hung a huge bell composed of straw and stalks, with a corn-and-pumpkin clapper. Every inch of the interior, as of all the roof-surfaces, excepting over the exhibits and corridors, was covered with corn and stalks.

The supporting posts of the building, which were many in number, were effective mediums for the display of ingenuity. The several sub-committees vied with each other in producing the most artistic effects with these. By a symmetrical laying on of corn some of the posts were changed into Ionic, Gothic, Doric and Corinthian columns, while others were laden with bouquets of tinted grasses and grains. Probably none of the visitors at the palace, up to that time, were aware of the charming shades and hues of corn husks. As decorative materials they rival the shades and hues in which every feminine heart finds such delight.

The ceilings above the booths were ornamented with devices which cannot be described in words so as to convey a suggestion of their appearance. Geometrical figures, artistic lines of grace and novel designs in combination of colors, were shown. It was a noticeable fact, frequently commented upon by observers, that the diversity of tastes displayed and the helpful rivalry of the workers in no instance resulted in disharmony. Everywhere was unity of action and concord of coloring. This is the more remarkable because of the lack of a grand design except that of spirit and desire. The booths

RESIDENCE GEO. D. PERKINS.

were not completed until just before the palace was thrown open and no committee knew precisely what the others were doing; yet when finished, all blended in harmonious effect.

The eye was bewildered on first seeing the interior of the palace and could detect the individual object only by repeated visits to the palace. It cannot be truthfully said that there was a superfluity of decoration, but a maze of curious and pleasing features. Turn which way you would, some new delight was offered to the vision. Here in this corner swayed a giant spider-web of strung kernels, with a huge spider resting watchfully in its meshes; there in that alcove was a stairway of golden grain, on the spiral steps of which a dainty doll stood, clothed in corn-husks of such delicacy that they appeared like silk; yonder, a landscape typifying the west, with sun of gold. Panels, ceilings, statuettes, lattices, curtains, all of corn. Flowers composed of husks and grains, but so skillfully made as to serve art's highest end. A flag of corn, bearing the legend: "Staff of Our Country;" a corn-stalk music staff with the notes to which all people sing "Praise God, from whom all blessings flow;" the humorous and the majestic paying tribute to the occasion. Emblems of husbandry and mottoes significant of the fertility of the land "The valleys also are covered with corn," "Sioux City never sleeps," etc., were disposed about the building. The Jackson street entrance was adorned with a screen upon which was worked a rustic scene and on the reverse side the inquiry, "Why not anchor in Sioux City?" the lettering being done in cereals, and the word "anchor" being represented by an exquisite anchor in colored grains.

SIOUX CITY JOURNAL BUILDING.

Miniature farm-yards, models of the Corn Palace, articles of wearing apparel, maps, pictures, stars, eagles, and a seemingly infinite variety of designs were presented to the admiring eye of the public. The originality of the decorators and exhibitors was amazing.

From these brief allusions to the display of products, which were so numerous and intricately arranged as to require far more space than is at command in this review, the reader will be able to form somewhat of an idea of the exposition. The Corn Palace was an educator. The thousands who saw it will not only be permanently benefitted by the revelation of new forms of art, but will also derive perpetual advantage from the expression, in comprehensive style, of the resources and magnitude of the region. No one could fail to receive enlarged impressions of the northwest and of Sioux City as the commercial capital of the northwest.

The rink building was decorated plainly with corn-stalks pendant from the ceilings and arranged about the sides. This hall was used for drills, band contests, concerts, public speaking and the final ball. While not especially ornamented, it was exceedingly essential to the carrying out of the programme of entertainments.

The principal streets of the city during Festival week were so finely decorated as to command a degree of admiration but little less than that bestowed on the Corn Palace itself. Chief among the features of the display were the illuminated arches, erected at the intersections of the main streets.

RESIDENCE DR. WM. R. SMITH.

These artificial structures consisted of huge spans and cross-trees, towering in pyramidal form to a height of fifty feet and each bearing about 300 jets covered with glass globes of assorted colors. Eight arches spanned Fourth street, which, viewed from the west, appeared like a stream of fire. Two miles of gas-pipe were required for this system of lighting, and there were over 8,000 jets. A massive and ornate arch, with thatched peaks and elaborate figures wrought in corn, spanned Pierce street between Fourth and Fifth streets. This, also, was illuminated at night with gas jets under glass globes.

It would require an enumeration of every business house and office in the city to describe the private decorations. From a simple veneering of corn in the ear to a complex and carefully drawn plan of artistic adornment, each building along the public thoroughfares was made to honor the event. The decorative mania burst forth in cumulative force. Gigantic ears of corn were built; arches, covered with stalks and pumpkins—a very effective material, by the way, in point of color—spanned the sidewalks; fronts of buildings were laid over with solid corn until no sign of brick or wood was visible; store windows were filled with symbolic figures and emblematic designs; clocks, mortars, shoes, anvils, pigs, villages, corn-fields, palaces, bonnets, hats, clothing, carpenters' tools, grocers' signs, statuettes of Ceres and King Corn, in fact every business, trade and calling was represented by some appropriate device in the windows and upon the streets. It may be said that the overflow of artistic zeal from the Corn Palace affected every man, woman and child in Sioux City and stirred each one to special effort in the work of beautifying the city.

It may be well here to give some account of the details of the Corn Palace Festival. It extended over one week, beginning October 3. The central feature, of course, was the Corn Palace itself, which excited extraordinary enthusiasm throughout the Northwest, and which the multitudes gathered in Sioux City never tired to gaze on. As the Palace approached completion in its beauty and uniqueness, the fame of it ran like wildfire, and it was manifest that there would be an immense concourse of visitors.

GORDON BLOCK.

Elaborate preparations were made for their entertainment illuminations, fireworks for each night, processions every day, band contests, military drills, races, etc. The programme in all particulars was carried out with an enthusiasm which rendered it even in result better than in anticipation.

The formal opening of the Corn Palace occurred on the evening of October 2. Crowds of delighted visitors thronged through the portals, and there was a dense press of people in Armory Hall, where the opening ceremony took place. Senator Charles H. Van Wyck, of Nebraska, the orator of the occasion, delivered an address appropriate to the place and all its suggestions. The following is an extract from the opening paragraphs of the address:

We cannot realize the amount of the corn crop, even when figuring the thousand million bushels raised annually; neither the empire of soil, with capacity unbounded, devoted to its growth We cannot realize as we stand in this grand and novel structure, the great wealth tributary to your beautiful city, and the rich area which finds its market at your doors. Iowa one of the youngest in the sisterhood, yet from her central position, the wonderful resources of her soil, the intelligence of her people, having sprung at one bound to the first rank and surpassed in the race many of her older sisters, bounded by two of the greatest rivers in the world—she lays a portion of her bounty at your feet. Northern Nebraska, so little known a few years ago, even by her neighbors, that a citizen of Iowa reported in Washington that it was impossible to build a railroad over her impassable mountains Northern Nebraska, at all events, only a few years ago a *terra incognita*, now behold in your midst the wonderful productions from a soil equal to that of Iowa, and brought here over railroads which traverse the former obstacles of impassable mountains that great country comes to rejoice and share the wealth of its prairies with you. Dakota--she has a double source of wealth in her boundless and exhaustless prairies and beneath the surface of her mountains and forests the precious metals which adorn this wonderful exhibition. Dakota, too, is tributary to your greatness and proud to bring her offering and unite in this dedication which stands as an augury that all this territory, without regard to state lines, looks upon your city as its great center, and that in the struggles which may come in the future you will stand shoulder to shoulder with them. More leagues away, where was the pastures-ground of the buffalo, from the ranges of Wyoming and Montana, come the descendants of the Shorthorns and Herefords, improved by the nutritious grasses and invigorating climate, to surpass the English stock, showing still further the wealth and vast territory which come to rejoice in this auspicious event.

Tuesday, October 1, dawned auspiciously. The weather, indeed, was all that could be desired until the last day of the week, when a drizzling rain intervened. Thousands of visitors from neighboring towns and villages began to arrive at an early hour. Throughout the forenoon regular and special trains packed with human freight arrived by all the lines of railroad. By 10 o'clock, when the first

RESIDENCE E. P. DEANE.

grand parade appeared to view, the crowd was so dense as to make locomotion almost impossible for a distance of ten blocks along Fourth street and for a considerable distance on the avenues leading thereto. Day after day the multitude that thronged the streets presented the same general aspect, save that it steadily increased in numbers. No such concourse of people was ever before seen in the Northwest.

The procession was announced on the programme as "A Grand Characteristic Parade, Representing Sioux City in 1854," and the promise was fulfilled. A more entertaining and significant presentment of historic fact would have been difficult to devise, and both to surviving pioneers of the Northwest whose memories retain the experiences of primitive life, and to the younger generation and to the visitors from the east to whom the hardships of early western days were known only by tradition, this opening display was, perhaps, the most interesting one shown during the festival.

The parade moved at 10 o'clock A. M., a platoon of police clearing the way, and after them, a band of musicians. Then came a band of Indians from the reservation—Omahas, Sioux and Winnebagos—numbering two hundred and fifty.   Seventy-five of the Indians were mounted, being in full war-paint and feather, and clad with the skins of wild animals, bright colored prints and gaudy cloths.   Uttering suppressed war-whoops and brandishing weapons as they moved along, there lacked nothing to paint the picture which

WOODBURY COUNTY COURT HOUSE.

in 1854 was one of terror to the adventurous settlers of the Northwest.   At some distance behind the troop of mounted warriors, which went through all the evolutions of Indian warfare - charging with piercing whoops, breaking in disorder, reforming with the precision of regular cavalry - there followed the remainder of the band in the motley vehicles and equipages which are only to be seen on an Indian reservation. The squaws and papooses were decked out in the gaudiest of savage fancy, and they gazed at the sights at every hand in wonderment equal to that with which they were themselves regarded by the multitude.

As the Indian band sped on and passed out of view, there came, most appropriately in the realistic panorama, the signs of advancing civilization, the representatives of the vanguard of the mighty army which drove out the red man and made his hunting ground a cornfield. The pack-train followed hard upon the heels of the retreating Indians—six ponies bearing a burden of furs and other frontier spoil, bound for the trading post. They, like the various other figures in this peculiar drama, were genuine. At their side was George Tackett, an experienced trapper in those wild days, who speaks the language of the native. He was clad in buckskin garb, with rifle slung for instant use, and looked like

RESIDENCE WM. L. JOY.

the frontiersman he used to be. If the pencil of a Stanley could have caught him then, historic art would have been enriched.

Next came the stage coach, with Tom Parrott, the second oldest stage driver in the Northwest, on the box. The stage contained express messengers, duly armed, and a "friendly" Indian.

The emigrant train of "the '50s" followed next. There was the spectacle of the old time "prairie schooners," drawn by oxen, and filled with the characteristic household effects, the working tools and scant possessions of the pioneer. Behind some wagons was the never-failing feed-box hung on, and over it the spinning wheel and venerable splint-bottomed chairs; in rear of others the family cow was led; the rear of another held a crate in which were ducks and chickens; one wagon had lost a hind wheel and came trailing along alone on a pole. The travel-stained canvas bore legends, copied from literal inscriptions remembered by the early comers.

The next picture was especially realistic, a freight train bound for the Black Hills camps. It was no illusion, for the immense vans had seen actual service. Three vans, lashed together in true frontier style, piled full of freight, were drawn by six-mule teams, the driver guiding them with a single line, and the bells upon their harness jingling merrily as they moved along. It was a true survivor of the old-time prairie life.

It would require too much space to describe particularly the "floats" and the various other representations of pioneer days which made up the first day's parade. What has been said will suffice as a suggestion of the comprehensiveness and accuracy of this particular display, and also of the other parades during the Festival.

On Wednesday morning the Industrial Parade occurred. On Thursday and Friday the crowd grew to prodigious proportions. The feature of Thursday morning's entertainment was the Military Parade,

SIOUX CITY LINSEED OIL WORKS.

and on Friday morning there was the Consolidated Review, while in the afternoon the Grand Lodge of Iowa Masons laid the corner stone of the Chamber of Commerce building. On Saturday night, October 8, the doors of the first Corn Palace were closed to the public.

But a day or two later, and before the building was torn down, two interesting events occurred. A party of eminent railroad men, composed of Cornelius Vanderbilt, Mr. Ferris, Albert Keep, Chauncey M. Depew, Marvin Hughitt, J. M. Whitman, Mr. Webb of the Wagner Car Company, Vice-President Sykes of the Northwestern system, Mr. DeCosta of the Lake Shore road and Mr. Fitch of the Sioux City and Pacific road, were traveling by special train over the lines in which they were interested and signified a desire to visit the Corn Palace. Although the exposition was then closed, the city authorities and a number of Sioux City business men received this party, in an informal manner, Monday morning, and conducted it through the Palace, still undisturbed in decorations and exhibits. The visitors expressed hearty appreciation of the evidences of the prosperity of this region. Mr. Depew was called on to address the company and spoke in his eloquent and felicitous style.

Two days later, President Cleveland and his party, then on a tour through the west and south, visited the Corn Palace. Although their route was through Sioux City, they had at an earlier day, because of lack of time and other engagements, declined to include a stop at Sioux City in their programme of the tour. The city council, business associations and management of the Corn Palace, had united in formal invitation to the President, but for the reasons named the invitation was not

RESIDENCE L. C. PETERS.   RESIDENCE J. T. CHESNEY.

favorably responded to. But after the President was well on his way to the west, the fame of the Palace was such that renewed invitation was accepted, although acceptance involved an interruption of the running schedule of the special train which bore the President's party. This was the only departure therefrom made by the President during his whole tour of the country, and the compliment to the Corn Palace was thus only the more significant.

On the clear and frosty morning of Wednesday, October 12, the train bearing the company of eminent personages arrived in Sioux City. Mayor Cleland, regarding the wishes of the President, informally received the party. A large concourse of citizens was present. The President and Mrs. Cleveland,

Mr. and Mrs. Postmaster-General W. F. Vilas, Judge Wilson Bissell, Col. Lamont, and others of the presidential party were assigned to carriages, and, escorted by a military company, were driven directly to the Corn Palace. The public were excluded from the building. Ladies of the Decorative Committee and a few invited guests were admitted.

The President and friends moved about the building, viewing the exhibits and decorations with evident interest. No speeches were made. Mr. Cleveland expressed surprise at the quality of the corn, and remarked that it certainly must be a rich country. He asked many questions relative to the productiveness and resources of the Northwest. His curiosity was aroused by specimens of parti-colored "Squaw Corn," and he said, "With your permission, I will take one of these," putting an ear of the corn in his pocket. Mrs. Cleveland was the recipient of numerous boquets and other souvenirs of the Palace.

The President's party remained in the Palace half an hour, engaged in pleasant conversation and unpretentious and admiring survey of the exposition, and was then escorted to the train, which at once departed.

ANDREWS, FLETCHER & CASE'S MILLS.

The visit of the President's party was, under the circumstances, a fair illustration of the interest which was excited throughout the country in the Festival. The leading papers of all the large cities sent special correspondents who daily telegraphed elaborate reports of its features and progress. The leading pictorial papers, like Harper's Weekly and Frank Leslie's in this country, and even the London Illustrated News, published copious illustrations and gave extended accounts.

Upon the departure of the President the Corn Palace of 1887 closed its doors. Workmen were soon engaged in tearing down the building and hundreds of souvenir-seekers were busy gathering mementoes of the great success.

THE CORN PALACE OF 1888.

The success of the Sioux City Corn Palace of 1887 was so signal, and the impression made by it upon the public mind so deep and abiding, that it became by virtue of its own force, a permanent and distinctive Sioux City enterprise. It was taken for granted by the tens of thousands of visitors who looked upon the first embodiment of the Corn Palace idea, and it was the common remark, that

Sioux City should be the scene of an annual harvest pageant upon the lines marked out or suggested by the Festival of 1887. Local aspiration answering to the earnest demand of the Northwest, involved this result, the interest of which running far beyond the limits of the Upper Missouri Valley enlists attention which may almost be described as national in extent.

In truth the portals of the Corn Palace of 1887 had not been finally closed upon the public before preparations began for the Corn Palace of 1888. A permanent organization to carry on the enterprise was at once mapped out. In the early spring the work was taken up anew and prosecuted with vigor. The enterprise was regularly incorporated under the laws of the State, the incorporators including the wealthiest and most prominent citizens, and capital ample for all purposes was promptly subscribed.

RESIDENCE W. P. PETTIT.　　　　RESIDENCE A. S. GARRETSON.

The plan for the Corn Palace of 1888 is identical in purpose with that of 1887, but it is incomparably more comprehensive in scope and more complete and elaborate in detail. The development of the plan this year is under circumstances entirely different from those surrounding the first Corn Palace. Then it was an unknown problem, every element of which was novel, and even the possibility of solution was at first in doubt. The Corn Palace association this year could walk in confidence in the light of the brilliant demonstration of last year. The rich results of its eminent experiences were the sure guides to a grander success. The discoveries of the decorative uses of the corn plant and of its families of the field were at once suggestions of the marvelous possibilities of the Corn Palace idea and an inspiring incentive to effort for their full realization.

The Corn Palace of 1888 is therefore both an improvement on and an enlargement of the Corn Palace of 1887. Wherever there was crudity it has been removed, wherever there was imperfection it has been corrected, and all the wonderful beauties and significance of the thought have been refined and adequately represented. It is not proposed to attempt to describe here in words the Corn Palace which will be opened

PEAVEY GRAND OPERA HOUSE AND CHAMBER OF COMMERCE.

to the public during the Festival of 1888, from September 24 to October 6, for the subject is one which written language is peculiarly inadequate to set forth. The drawing of the Corn Palace of 1888, which is given on a former page of this publication, affords, in a general way, suggestion of the contour and proportions of the exterior of the structure. The architecture may be loosely described as of the pavilion style, airy and graceful, and original in combination as it is unique in purpose, requiring for its best effect the rich blending and contrasts of the colors of the natural products with which it is decorated. The structure is firmly built, with strong walls and tight roof, and with a view to the comfort of visitors in any weather. With ground dimensions of 150 by 150 feet, the edifice affords ample interior space for the splendid adornments and substantial displays which it will contain. The interior will be disposed in an entirely different manner from that of the first palace—with spacious courts and corridors and galleries, as well as retiring rooms and toilet conveniences and all the other arrangements necessary to its purpose and to the accommodation of the public.

RESIDENCE E. R. SMITH.

The Corn Palace itself, though the central and characteristic feature of the Festival, will be surrounded with many accessories to heighten its interest. All the principal features of the first Corn Palace Festival will be expanded and perfected, and the programme includes also many new and capital attractions. The novel scheme of public illumination, which was so notable a feature of the Festival of 1887, will be carried out on a far more extensive scale. One of the most pleasing incidents of the occasion will be the elaborate spectacles presented by the grand parades, illustrative of subjects appropriate to the time and place, which will occur on the several days of the Festival. For these especial preparation has been made upon a plan in which expense and effort were not considered as obstacles. In addition the programme includes features which run the whole gamut of popular amusements and sports—races and excursions; the marshalling of the full military strength of the Northwest and competitive drills between the various companies; a grand showing of musical associations; the pageantry of civic and benevolent organizations; pyrotechnic displays; the formal opening of the Peavey Grand Opera House, the corner-stone of which was laid during the Festival of 1887, etc., etc. In short, the design and preparations are such as to make full draft upon, as well as to illustrate, the resources of Sioux City and the Northwest, insuring an entertainment so distinctive in character and so grand in method as to take rank as an event of national interest, and to be verily a carnival expressive of the satisfaction of a great people.

The success of the Corn Palace Festival of 1888 is more than assured. It is certified by the eminent success of the first Corn Palace in 1887. That remarkable achievement was the result of effort compressed within a few weeks, against unfavorable circumstances which have already been described, whereas the opportunities of a whole year of preparation and the light of fruitful experience are behind

RESIDENCE J. L. FOLLETT.

the Corn Palace of 1888. Moreover, in the agricultural domain of the Upper Missouri Valley there has been a season of prosperity which, this year, even beyond the generous bounty of ordinary seasons, accentuates the significance of the Corn Palace. Seed-time and harvest, which never fail in the unrivaled Corn Region of the Northwest about Sioux City, have been propitious, and the yield of corn and grain and every growth rejoices the heart and moves to celebration.

To such a prospect Sioux City extends a cordial invitation to the world, and to the million visitors who will gaze upon the Corn Palace of 1888, assurance of their fullest satisfaction.

www.ingramcontent.com/pod-product-compliance
Lightning Source LLC
Chambersburg PA
CBHW032046090426
42733CB00030B/716